Filming Stop-Motion Animation

By Zoë Wilkinson Saldaña

CHERRY LAKE Publishing

Published in the United States of America by
Cherry Lake Publishing
Ann Arbor, Michigan
www.cherrylakepublishing.com

Series Editor: Kristin Fontichiaro
Reading Adviser: Marla Conn, MD, Ed., Literacy Specialist,
Read-Ability, Inc.
Photo Credits: All photos by Zoë Wilkinson Saldaña

Library of Congress Cataloging-in-Publication Data
Names: Saldaña, Zoë Wilkinson, author.
Title: Filming stop-motion animation / by Zoë Wilkinson Saldaña.
Description: Ann Arbor, Michigan : Cherry Lake Publishing, [2018] | Series: Makers
    as innovators junior | Series: 21st century skills innovation library | Series: Makers
    as innovators junior | Includes bibliographical references and index.
Identifiers: LCCN 2017029316 | ISBN 9781534107786 (lib. bdg.) | ISBN 9781534109766
    (pdf) | ISBN 9781534108776 (pbk.) | ISBN 9781534120754 (ebook)
Subjects: LCSH: Animation (Cinematography)—Juvenile literature. | Stop-motion animation
    films—Juvenile literature.
Classification: LCC TR897.6 .S35 2018 | DDC 777/.7—dc23
    LC record available at https://lccn.loc.gov/2017029316

Cherry Lake Publishing would like to acknowledge the work of the Partnership for
21st Century Learning. Please visit *www.p21.org* for more information.

Printed in the United States of America
Corporate Graphics

A Note to Adults: Please review the instructions for the activities in this book before allowing children to do them. Be sure to help them with any activities you do not think they can safely complete on their own.

A Note to Kids: Be sure to ask an adult for help with these activities when you need it. Always put your safety first!

Table of Contents

Some cows dream of being movie stars.

The Magic of Stop-Motion

Who are the main characters in your favorite movie? Sometimes the main characters are people just like you. Other times, they might be cars, talking animals, or even LEGO figures. What if you made a movie where the characters were toys and other objects from around your house?

What Is Stop-Motion?

Stop-motion is a type of **animation**. It is created by taking many photographs. After each photo, the animator moves the characters just a little bit. This process is repeated over and over. At the end, the photos are used to make a movie.

In stop-motion movies, the rules of everyday life don't apply. This cow is so excited that its eyes pop through the binoculars!

Let's Make a Movie!

This book will walk you through the steps of making your first stop-motion movie. Most stop-motion movies are just a few seconds long. This is because you must take photographs for every second of the movie. This takes a lot of time, so be **patient** as you work.

Why Eight Images Per Second?

You can choose how many images, or frames, to use in each second of your movie. Using more frames makes the movie look smoother. It takes longer to film, though.

Who do you want to star in your movie? A favorite old toy is a great choice.

Creating Your Characters

What should your characters look like? What will they do and say? You can create a stop-motion movie starring any object you have nearby. Turn your favorite toys into movie stars. Open the fridge and make a movie about fruits and vegetables. The choice is yours!

Clay Animation

One of the most popular kinds of stop-motion animation is called clay animation. With clay animation, an animator molds pieces of clay into characters. The clay is soft. This means the animator can move it in any direction. Characters can walk around or even change their faces.

Gather all of the supplies you'll need before you start filming.

Gather Your Materials

Here are a few things you'll need to get started:

- Objects to be characters in your movie
- Pencil and paper
- Smartphone or tablet with a stop-motion animation app installed
- Small cardboard box
- Desk lamp
- Stand to hold the smartphone or tablet steady

Grab your pen and paper and draw your storyboard. It's okay if you end up changing it later.

Plan Your Storyboard

You have an idea and a few characters. Now it's time to plan your movie! A **storyboard** is a guide that shows what will happen in your movie. It helps you imagine what the finished movie will look like. Make a storyboard with three drawings. You will draw the beginning, middle, and end of your animation.

Try asking yourself what you want your objects to do. These eyes pop wide open in a funny way.

Build Your Set

When filming a movie, it helps to make a **set** behind your characters. All you need is a cardboard box. Maybe you have a shoebox somewhere. You could also use a tissue box. Add drawings to the set to make it more colorful.

Make your movie indoors with a lamp shining on your set. This will keep the scene free of shadows.

Set Up Your Equipment

Now it's time to film your movie. You will need a smartphone or tablet with a stop-motion animation app installed. Ask an adult for help if you need it. You also need a way to keep the smartphone or tablet from moving as you work. Some devices have cases with built-in stands. You can also use a **tripod** if you have one. Or try sticking your device into a full roll of toilet paper. That will keep it in place.

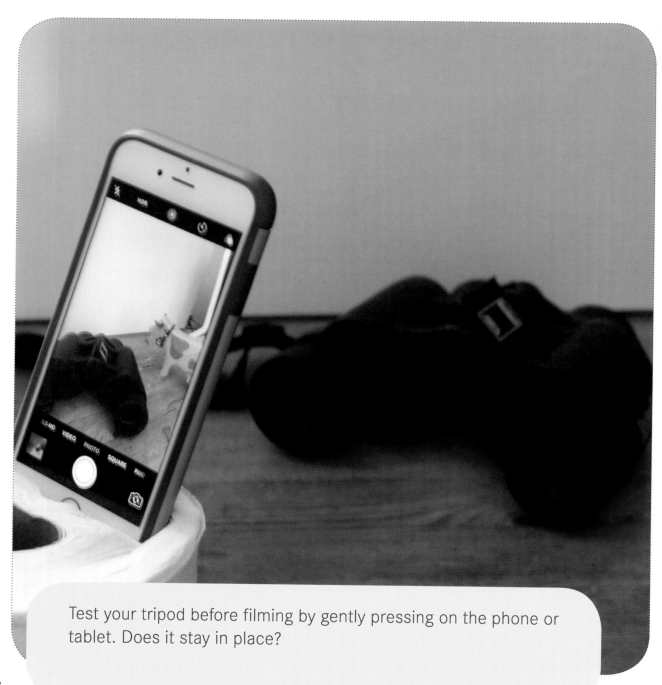

Test your tripod before filming by gently pressing on the phone or tablet. Does it stay in place?

Shoot Your Scene

Every second of your movie is broken up into eight smaller moments. Do you want a character to spin around in one second? Then you'll need to take eight photos. Move the character one-eighth of the way each time. The stop-motion app will combine these photos into a movie.

Stop-Motion Movie Apps

There are several free stop-motion apps you can use. For an Android device, look for *PicPac Stop Motion & TimeLapse*. For an iPhone or iPad, try *Stop Motion Studio*. See the app's "About" or "Help" section if you have questions. You can also ask an adult to help you look up information online.

Once you are done taking photos, click on the "export movie" option to save your movie.

Edit Your Movie

The movie should now be saved to your phone or tablet. Congratulations, you're a **director**! Try making even more movies. Next time you can use different characters or a new set. You could even try making characters out of clay. It's up to you and your imagination!

Glossary

animation (an-uh-MAY-shuhn) the process of turning drawings, photos, or computer-made images into a movie

director (duh-REK-tur) someone who oversees the making of a movie

patient (PAY-shuhnt) able to put up with problems without getting upset

storyboard (STOR-ee-bord) a plan for filming a movie that usually includes drawings of what will appear on-screen in each shot

set (SET) the location where characters are filmed in a movie

tripod (TRYE-pahd) a three-legged device on which a camera can be mounted

Find Out More

Books

Masura, Shauna. *Record It! Shooting and Editing Digital Video*. Ann Arbor, MI: Cherry Lake Publishing, 2013.

Trueit, Trudi Strain. *Animation*. Ann Arbor, MI: Cherry Lake Publishing, 2009.

Web Sites

Brickfilms.com
http://brickfilms.com
This website will help you learn how to make animations using LEGO bricks. It also includes lessons on topics such as using sound in animations.

How to Draw for Kids
www.artforkidshub.com/how-to-draw
Want to improve your storyboard drawings? This site gives you lessons for drawing all kinds of things. This will help you prepare for your stop-motion movies!

Instructables: How to Make an Awesome Claymation
www.instructables.com/id/How-to-Make-an-Awesome-Claymation
This guide teaches how to use clay to make a clay animation movie. Clay lets you explore new ways for your characters to show emotions and move around!

Index

About the Author

Zoë is a writer and researcher living in Ann Arbor, Michigan. She loves to learn about the surprising and wonderful things kids create with technology. Most days, Zoë can be found going on hikes, writing, or playing video games.